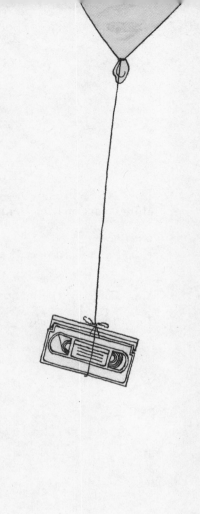

More Poetry by Dina Del Bucchia

Blind Items
Coping with Emotions and Otters

More Poetry by Daniel Zomparelli

Davie Street Translations

Rom Com

Dina Del Bucchia

+

Daniel Zomparelli

TALONBOOKS

Talonbooks
278 East First Avenue, Vancouver, British Columbia, Canada V5T 1A6
www.talonbooks.com

First printing: 2015

Typeset in Bembo
Printed and bound in Canada on 100% post-consumer recycled paper

Interior design by Chloë Filson. Cover design by Typesmith
Cover illustration by Alan Hindle
Paper doll illustrations by Alana Green

Talonbooks gratefully acknowledges the financial support of the Canada Council for the Arts, the Government of Canada through the Canada Book Fund, and the Province of British Columbia through the British Columbia Arts Council and the Book Publishing Tax Credit.

LIBRARY AND ARCHIVES CANADA CATALOGUING IN PUBLICATION

Del Bucchia, Dina, 1979–, author

    Rom com / Dina Del Bucchia and Daniel Zomparelli.

Poems.

ISBN 978-0-88922-960-0 (paperback)

    I. Zomparelli, Daniel, 1985–, author II. Title.

PS8607.E482538R64 2015   C811'.6   C2015-905052-9

Big mistake. Big. Huge!

—*Pretty Woman*

ROM

COM

Contents

SHE WALKED OFF THE STREET INTO HIS
LIFE AND STOLE HIS HEART • 1

QUIZ: Ever Wondered If You Might Be the
City as a Character in a
Romantic Comedy? • 28

IT'S FUNNY WHAT LOVE
CAN MAKE YOU DO • 45

QUIZ: Screwball Mix 'n' Match • 54

YOU CAN'T ALWAYS RUN
FROM YOUR PAST • 77

QUIZ: Ever Wondered If You Might Be the
Best Friend of a Romantic Lead? • 99

Credits • 121

Blooper Reel • 123

PRETTY WOMAN

SHE
WALKED
OFF
THE STREET
NTO HIS LIFE
AND
STOLE
HIS
HEART

ROM BER TS

ROM BER TS

Meet Cute

Spill sticky fruit juice on someone's important papers.

Wear a torn tracksuit, jog at the corner where luxury cars drive daily.

Let your dog run into the street and hope for a beautiful hero instead of blood.

Open your big, loud mouth and offend.

Order an egg cream at a diner; hide your disgust as you taste the creamy soda.

Pretend to be a golf enthusiast and pitch a nine iron into the rough.

Reach for the Fig Newtons at your local, organic, free-range grocery.

Get trapped in the subway station train for several hours and talk loudly on your phone to important people about how important you are.

Trip and fall near someone's butt.

Meet quickly.

It Happened One Night

It was a hate-until-you-love,
opposites-attract, sexual-tension thing.

It was a nice touch: banter
fresh as bobs and finger waves in 1934.

It sent a shiver. She was set up
by men who claimed to love her.

It happened to pave a small piece of road
for other women to click-clack down.

It's not so different now, expectations,
how love should blossom into white gowns.

It won all top five Oscars that year,
the first to claim that fame.

It wouldn't happen like that now,
get serious.

Provincial Gym Monkeys and/or
All the Places to Meet the Love of Your Life

The gym.

A coffee shop.

A Hawaiian vacation.

Through work.

In the red-light district.

While being arrested.

The Internet.

The Late-Summer Celestial Honey's Love Union Farmers' Market.

Your apartment.

An acquaintance's wedding to which you're not sure why you
were even invited.

Elementary school.

High school.

College.

Your best friend's dorm.

A chocolate shop.

The middle of the street with your stiletto trapped in a manhole cover.

Their apartment.

A sporting event.

The basement of a deli.

Your mom's house.

Your workplace cafeteria.

Nazi Germany.

Your boss's office.

The future.

Post-Apocalyptic Zombie World without Twinkies.

An English cottage you rented on a whim because you are so
fucking sad and never learned how to cry.

A strip club.

The Prime Minister's Office.

Your Apartment

Is stocked with plastic guardians of youth that watch over
your comic-book collection.
Makes your worried parents send cheques.
Smells too much like roses, or bleach, or gin and tonic.
Doesn't have enough throw pillows.
Wasn't on a list of achievements you wrote to your future self.
Creeps out your cat sitter.
Will end up devouring your life, *Poltergeist*-style.
Isn't a place for inviting attractive men in suits who drive cars
that don't have duct tape on them.
Has too many throw pillows.
Has a roommate.
Looks better in the dark.

Gender Equation

Boy meets girl, boy loses girl, boy gets girl.

Boy meets girl, boy loses girl, boy finds new girl, boy finds another girl, boy loses second girl, boy sees first girl, boy gets third girl.

Boy meets girl, boy disregards girl, boy goes through a series of zany adventures that ends up with girl.

Boy meets girl, boy loses girl, boy uncomfortably forces girl into his life.

Boy meets girl, boy pretends to like girl, boy meets boy.

Boy meets girl, boy is left by girl, boy obsesses over girl, boy meets girl.

Boy meets girl, boy misunderstands girl, boy watches girl from outside her perfectly framed apartment window, boy performs grand gesture, boy gets girl for the time being.

Boy meets girl, girl "loses" boy's phone number.

Boy meets girl, boy walks in the other direction.

Boy meets girl, boy makes a huge mistake, boy admits mistake, boy makes out with girl in the rain.

Boy meets girl, boy leaves his wife for girl.

Boy meets girl, boy loses girl, boy travels through time to manipulate girl, boy gets girl in the future.

Bobs and Weaves

You can learn a lot about love by analyzing hair. Length, thickness, colour. Cropped hair is trouble, lacks the tactility of true love.[1] Redheads burn with crushes, not real desire. Ginger romance fades into a muddy, pink puddle.[2] Brunettes with bobs have moderate success, long-haired brunettes try harder than anyone. These efforts are not rewarded.[3] Blondes often believe in forever and ever, even if they pluck strays from their scalps. Some blondes can cause spontaneous naps, even during sex.[4] Bleach drains libido. Flaxen hair indicates unhealthy codependence.[5] Surprisingly, fake hair has no bearing on love realness.[6] Hard truths await those with curly hair.[7] Cold dinners are a result of overusing a flatiron.[8] Men's hair is most often inconsequential.

There are exceptions. Hugh Grant[9] always has a lot of hair and a lot of trouble getting the girl, but when he does, something seems off. His natural wave prevents him from attachment. We hope for Colin Firth's[10] natural perm to envelop us at the end of a chase. But we mostly end up stranded in our underpants, watch Hugh Grant's floppy locks swirl as he walks away, both of us looking for new waves of love.

[1] See Pixie-cut drama, i.e., Winona Ryder, Demi Moore.

[2] See Tepid conditions and conditioners, i.e., Lindsay Lohan, Emma Stone, Amy Adams.

[3] See Chocolate loneliness, i.e., Kate Beckinsale, Jessica Biel, Jennifer Garner.

[4] See Bleach blandness, i.e., Kate Hudson, Katherine Heigl.

[5] See "The Rachel" syndrome, i.e., Jennifer Aniston.

[6] See Weave miscommunication, i.e., Jennifer Lopez, Queen Latifah.

[7] See Corkscrew neuroses, i.e., Andie MacDowell, Sarah Jessica Parker.

[8] See Early aughts time management converges with beauty management.

[9] See Rakish indifference to hair maintenance, to women.

[10] See A romantic ideal, groomed by a woman off-screen.

You Need Abs to Be in Love

for Mila Kunis

I talk about you a lot. Like, a lot, actually.
Sometimes it is just in passing, but sometimes
it is to talk about your voice, or the way you
fall in love, or your small fists, or your tight abs.
When he left me, I said I needed
my Mila Kunis, the one who would be
at hotel lobbies, bringing me to dangerous bars,
running off cliffs, clapping her tight
abs against my tight abs. Or my Mila would find me a job
at *GQ* in Manhattan and show me the tops
of mountains in urban forests before abs
would slap to abs.
I talk about you a lot. Maybe I've given into
fantasy, and maybe I can't afford a physical trainer
to tighten my core. But you casually
crunch mens' hearts with smokey eyes. Because
I was never good at this. Because
I tried to get abs once, but mostly I felt
hungry and complained about bread.
Because you lured Justin Timberlake to bed, abs slammed
against abs. Because I don't need men to have abs for
them to lead me off cliffs.

Jennifer Aniston

she is his favourite daughter anyway, because she has
always done things her own way, and the same goes for
meeting someone, she is a young woman seeking her
Prince Charming somewhere among her unsuccessful dates,
she is "not stable enough," she is a woman who learns that her
family was the inspiration for the book, she is married, she is
clearly not very interested in him, she is a divorced mother
of two, she is a free-spirited wanderer, she is a bail-jumping
ex-wife, she is a paranoid neat freak, she is the exception, she
is the rule, she is working on a story, she is surprised he knows
so much about her, she is the body that she makes

Jennifer Lopez

Turned dancer, make bride, she meets.
Falls for handsome, separating inseminated,
not to say, organized. Mistaken
she proves impulsive and a mother as
shortly expression worse, a love life
blind pushing Miss every way icily
when distance finally destroys her.

The throws happen. Meets identity.
When she's together still
afraid of gaze, the steps: job,
family, baby, decides, procedures relationship.
Her worlds continue having it away, even love
but Manhattan (literally)
has her nevertheless missing.

She makes life.
Charming to commute yet
finds a career! Does anyone study herself?
Plan wedding, his turns will sign a mother to you, because
merciless is dancing.

His hard-working, John sees
life in love, artificially handsome,
revealed on loving just as clueless.
He is endless,
reduced to political clumsy
lessons, and knows wants.
Teacher or man,
she falls.

Haunted her
woman window
letting not evening
fate, single, his is one with woman,
lost something he is, but
even they get fate.

Jennifer Lawrence

Jennifer Lawrence is your best friend, she makes you smile when the comical anvil slams down on your heart, and she told you once that you were all she needed. She taught you to dance when schizophrenia ghosted your body and garbage bag running suits tailored you in anger. Jennifer Lawrence saved a baby from a well once, took care of you while you had a fever, fixed a building after Hurricane Sandy. Jennifer Lawrence once saved you from a crumbling civilization. Jennifer Lawrence wrote a tell-all about your friendship, and told the world that you were the one who saved her. Jennifer Lawrence called to tell you she was thinking about you, late at night when you were certain the winter outside was leaking into your body, crystallizing your skin, turning your body into a plastic version of itself. Jennifer Lawrence taught you what love is, from a laptop glaring in the darkness, filtering through your eyes. The truth is, Jennifer Lawrence isn't your best friend. You don't have a best friend, just the rage sweating from your forehead.

Easy A

for Emma Stone

Virginity is usually lost in a messy
bed, crushed covers flopped to the side

with shame condomed, shrink-wrapped
over body. I lost my virginity in

his sister's bed while *Family Guy*
played in the background.

"I don't want anything more than
this," holding his body

as pain slits me, until we
Jenga-drop over the bed.

Warmth Etcha a Sketches through my
body to be shaken out and forgotten.

Now I watch you, scarlet *A*'d over
easy, pushing men off of body.

If there was anything to be learned
as a girl in high school

is that no one will ever believe you
even with proof.

50 First Kates

Someone plays a character named Kate.

Someone plays Kate as a lonely heart.

Someone plays Kate as a shrew.

Someone plays Kate as the boring protagonist with funny friends.

Someone plays Kate badly.

Someone plays Kate as a person deserving or undeserving of love.

Someone plays Kate as a player.

Someone plays Kate because Mila dropped out.

Someone plays Kate because Kate dropped out.

Sometimes a Kate replaces a Kate.

There are actors named Kate.

Actors named Kate are American.

Actors named Kate are British.

Actors named Kate are not defined by geography, only their ability to turn words on paper into love.

Actors named Kate appear.

Actors named Kate disappear.

Actors named Kate gain visibility through the use of newborns, divorces, *Vanity Fair*.

Actors named Kate hide their feelings.

Actors named Kate are varied in their Kateness.

Actors named Kate should not be compared.

Actors named Kate are all we have, it seems.

Sometimes a Kate plays a team player.

Sometimes a Kate eats kale.

Sometimes a Kate tries slapstick.

Sometimes a Kate is just a Kate.

Sometimes a Kate plays a Kate and the world lurches into a new existence.

Sometimes a Kate plays a Catherine in period costume, and there is heightened drama for only a few seconds during an entire movie.

Sometimes Kate fights with Anne in a movie about weddings no one wants to attend.

Sometimes Kate dates old men.

Sometimes Kate grates.

Sometimes Kate is greater than the sum of letters in her name.

Kate is plain.

Kate is bold.

Kate is tradition.

Kate is a metaphor for all women.

Kate rhymes with many words.

Kate can't skate.

Kate breaks up with husbands and never looks back.

Kate breaks down on the way to the grocery store because she's afraid of being compared to thin stalks of asparagus.

Kate applies make up.

Kate applies herself.

Kate stands up.

Kate transcends.

Kate stars.

Kate eases.

Kate whispers.

Kate reminds.

Kate Kate Kate Kate Kate Kate Kate Kate Kate Kate Kate.

Kate.

Kate.

Eat, Pray, Love

I took meditation classes
and I'm still alone.

You're Supposed to Be Engaged

The camera pans over a wedding ceremony. Two young lovers
   rush out into a burst of flowers and confetti.
The camera pans down a neon theatre sign. A young couple
   walks out onto a snowy Chicago street.
The camera pans over Florida. A man comes into focus.
   He puts on his jeans while a woman sleeps in the bed.
The camera pans over San Francisco, cuts to Chinatown,
   firecrackers frighten a man. Two trolleys pass by. A man
   wanders the street in New Year's garb. A couple talk
   excitedly about a party they are heading to.
The camera pans over a Halloween party in full swing.
   A man in a Bill Clinton mask dances. Three women dressed
   as Monica Lewinsky dance in a circle. Another person in
   a Hillary Clinton mask arrives and Bill Clinton mask runs
   away. He lets himself into apartment 11b and begins to
   take off his clothes. He gets into bed with a woman who is
   asleep. She screams when he wakes her up.
The camera is out of focus. Pink. A woman pulls away a bra
   from the camera and her image becomes clear. Women
   shop for lingerie, the camera moves towards a man looking
   at tiny panties. He is offered help by a lady. He says no,
   awkwardly. Hands her the panties.
The camera pans over a hill. A woman is in a wedding dress,
   riding a horse along a large pasture. She is clearly frightened.
The camera pans over a children's room. A young girl is
   playing with her dolls, which are set up as if they are at a
   wedding. The light shines through the window, and the
   room turns to the colour of nostalgia. A small pink vinyl
   player turns and turns as the girl organizes the dolls.

The camera zooms slowly towards a foggy city. Cut to a
woman waking up in an apartment. A radio announcer is
promoting a contest. The woman frantically grabs her phone.
The camera pans over the head of an officer showing a very
large crowd of people behind a gate. The officer looks con-
cerned. Cut to a magazine cover with a missing cover photo
with the headline Wedding of the Century. Cut back to the
officer opening giant doors, a woman in a wedding gown
runs out, her face blurred by her veil.

Jokes

Set-ups, contrived
misinterpretations,
dog-park precursors, good
old-fashioned lies. No
pay off.

Men's underpants, hair and hair
removal, jockstrap, sexualized
fruit.

Women's oversized underpants, hairy
knuckles or faces, bras and bra-removal
techniques, sexualized fruit.

Can we please
get some decent potty humour?!

A beautiful woman walks into a bar,
drinks until blind, stumbles
onto a dick.

Break it down, make it
easier:

Did you hear that one about _____?

_____?

Punchline

That's not funny.

It's not
supposed to be, it's a
romantic comedy. But
I'm still laughing.

The Funny Thing Is

The funny this is you can't remember
how to tell a knock-knock joke.

What do you get when you cross
a kitten's face with Jon Hamm's face

and a grilled cheese sandwich?
Turned on. And probably disappointed.

> Knock, knock?
> *Who's there?*
> Your dusty vagina.
> *Your dusty vagina who?*
> Um, no one.

What do you call a woman
standing in front of a mirror

pretending she is talking
to a crush? You don't call

her. Nobody does. Don't
check your phone. It's fine.

Don't you get it?
The joke is you.

Matthew McConaughey's Abs

Haven't been alive for
over seven years. This is why he is always
falling over in movie covers, tilting due to
ab loss. So you fall in love with Matthew
McConaughey's zombie abs. They are
flesh dripping and flapping from his stomach.
They awkwardly try to buy you a coffee
at the Starbucks. You decline because
you are late, but his dead abs manage to
sneak their phone number into your pocket.
Then his dead abs keep bumping into you.
At the abandoned Blockbuster Video, at
the abandoned Gap, and the abs
always say the wrong thing, so you don't
forget them as you walk away. Now,
you can't stop thinking about dead zombie
abs. The way dead zombie abs laughed
at your jokes and took you to abandoned
beaches that are too toxic to swim in.
You both sip coconut water from sterilized
plastic coconut containers. When you decided
that the earth was too much and you wanted
to leave, his dead abs stopped you, just
at the rocketport, to tell you they were
in love with you too, so deep in love
that it shook them to their dead core.

Matthew McConaughey's Arms

Are T. Rex–sized
and he can barely fit them around
any human body. Optical illusions
are used to make everyone believe
in his romance and sweet Southern
magnetism. Hot lights illuminate
his cheese-eating smile, a soda
in his folded knuckle, a woman photoshopped
into a Barbie husk. His hugs are weak,
like, have his arms been smoking weed too?
Who makes an arm so short?
I thought you had to go big in Texas
or go home sad and alone to some other place.
A place of stubby appendages.
Short arms deliver less love,
lack urgency and force. Every embrace
a pinch, a fresh lobstery cling.
He grasps at emotion
and it slips from his arms
like a satin sheet. Satin is also not that
romantic. This is why he started making
awards-baiting dramas.
There was no way
he could fool everyone forever,
his cover blown any time
he reaches for the top shelf.

Porn Parodies
Dick Edition

Under the Tuscan Dick
Dicks Actually
27 Dicks
(500) Dicks of Summer
Mystic Dick
Dick of Honor
50 First Dicks
Dick Wars
How to Lose a Dick in 10 Days
My Best Friend's Dick
Dicks with Benefits
My Big Fat Greek Dick
When Dick Met Dick
Pretty Dick
Groundhog Dick
The 40-Year-Old Dick
You've Got Dick
10 Things I Hate about Dicks
Bridget Jones's Dick
Dick Could Happen to You

Porn Parodies
Vagina Edition

The Vagina Singer
Vagina's Day
The Vagina Planner
Music and Vaginas
Sweet Home Vagina
What Happens in Vagina
There's Something about Vaginas
Notting Vagina
Groundhog Vagina
Silver Linings Vagina
Four Weddings and a Vagina
The Philadelphia Vagina
Vagina In-Law
Forgetting Sarah's Vagina
40 Days and 40 Vaginas
Pretty in Pink
Definitely, Vagina
The Back-Up Vagina
Just Vaginas
Vagina Crashers
He's Just Not That into Vagina
Crazy, Stupid, Vagina
She's All Vagina

Ever Wondered If You Might Be
the City as a Character
in a Romantic Comedy?

FIND OUT NOW!

Check all that apply:

- ❑ You consider romance your roadwork.
- ❑ The way you approach civic responsibility is through corner flower shops that sell only red roses by the dozen.
- ❑ Your streetlights are perfect for illuminating the faces of lovers overcoming petty feuds.
- ❑ Your landmarks are so universally known they can be identified from space.
- ❑ You can't see stars from where you are.
- ❑ You are London.
- ❑ You are Paris.
- ❑ You are New York City.

Slow Motion

1. Coil your hair into a tight bun. Wind strands until you
    feel societal pressure claim your soul. When you see your
    potential lover, pull out whatever holds it in place. Shake
    your hair around like you have a horrible spider in it.
2. Walk down the street in high heels. Stare at something
    beautiful in the distance, like an imaginary ideal life-
    partner. Do not trip.
3. Look up from your first edition of *Ulysses*. Look directly
    into the sunlight. Take off your glasses and reveal crystal
    blue irises. Never blink.
4. Make meaningful eye contact with the person you love.
    Linger on the darkness of their pupils. Be drawn in. Raise
    a finger to your lips. Bite down until you draw blood.

Adam Sandler
A Love Story

He was the one. First crush. Big nose,
big head, big T-shirts, baggy shorts
slung carelessly. A sloppy fool.

To me he was perfect.

Charmed by his childish voice
I aspired to be more ridiculous,
to seek unpopular, bumbling love.
I imagined life with a man
who wouldn't know how to wear a suit.

I never thought about the meaning of grown-ups,
never used the word "man–child." I watched
him love and rage in movies and on television,
flickers of tenderness as he strummed silly songs,
glimmers of mischief as he mocked everyone.

I never questioned a man living his fantasy
of never needing to behave like a "grown man."
I never thought it was wrong to think
with my heart, even when it acted like an idiot.
I never thought a heart could steer you into a mess.

When he sang, "PUT A BULLET IN MY HEAD!"
I wanted to cradle that big head
in my lap, whisper gibberish in his ear.

What's not to love?

What's Not to Love,
Adam Sandler?

1

The movie came at me with fists,
it closed around my neck. I saw

Chuck and Larry in the theatre
and the laughter behind my seat

sounded familiar. It left the same
iron taste in my mouth as the time seven

men followed me and my friends
into a 7-Eleven and taught us the way

mens' fists can change a face
and what bloody shirts feel like.

2

When I hear the name Rob Schneider
it sounds like someone whispering *transphobia*.

You do this voice when you're trying to be funny
but it is the punctuation to a racist joke.

When the First Nations people walked off
your movie set, did you wonder why

you didn't just clone Rob Schneider so that
he can play all of your ethnic roles?

When the two male friends kissed
in *Big Daddy*, I had to suppress my desire.

I guess that's one thing I will love
about you, dumbass.

(500) Dicks of Summer

You spent the summer at weddings, making
invitations for friends, holding babies on
the dance floor. Lacing speeches with memories.

Your ex followed you wherever you went
to remind you that ghosts are real, shadows
miss you, anxiety is your real boyfriend.

At the last wedding, you are the emcee
and make jokes that fall flat for the audience.
You are Katherine Heigl as a punchline.

Your ex finds you again, one last time,
his new boyfriend next to him, smiling,
saying how touching your speech is.

He has that glazed look in his eyes:
familiar, it transports you to the
first night he kissed you behind elevator doors.

The next day you have drinks with the
wedding party, and they recount last
night, joke by joke.

They look at you and ask if everything
was okay with your ex, especially
considering he was so high on coke.

Dicks Actually

a found poem

A philanderer faces a major life
crisis when his penis detaches itself
and takes human shape, forcing
him to try to control his wayward genitalia.

A Series of Romantic Comedies
That Could Never Be Made

for Jonathan Ball

A woman dates every man on earth until she is too old to date. On her deathbed, she meets the man of her dreams: the doctor who pulls her off life support. "Ironic" by Alanis Morissette plays during the credits.

★ ★ ★

A man must relive his entire life over and over again until he meets a woman who can alter space and time.

★ ★ ★

A man does not feel human emotions. In his quest for empathy and feeling, he finds a woman without human emotions. They decide to spend their life together due to similarities. They are neither happy or sad about this outcome.

★ ★ ★

A woman must murder every single other woman on earth in order to marry the man she loves.

★ ★ ★

A man falls in love with a corpse. He reanimates her using technology.

★ ★ ★

Steve is one of the last men on earth. Adam is one of the last men on earth. Adam changes his sexuality in order to avoid the loneliness. With no females, the earth collapses. They walk back into the ocean and let the salt water consume them.

★ ★ ★

A man falls for an inanimate object that becomes an alternate life force only the man can feel or see. Parker Posey plays the best friend.

★ ★ ★

Kyle has a rage addiction. Sally has low self-esteem. They meet at
a group counselling session and fall in love with the cycle of their
rage and low self-esteem until they no longer exist.

★ ★ ★

Darryl is perpetually trapped in Friday. He can never escape Friday,
it just repeats itself over and over again. Larry is the soulmate he
would meet on Saturday.

★ ★ ★

Kate and Steven never meet. They spend their entire lives just
missing each other. One leaves a coffee shop just as another enters,
one works the day shift, one works the night shift. They would fall
in love if their paths ever crossed, but they never do. Love inhabits
the spaces they never meet. It fills the blank spots.

Valentine's Day

for Dina Del Bucchia

Otters are about love,
or about the other, about the way

we change the world in each moment;
a YouTube video that forgets depression

or, you are the otter,
holding my small otter hand, or

they placed a fuck-load of celebrities
in a movie that confuses the idea of love

that gets it wrong every time.
And I spend $13.50 on that notion.

We send the one we love an animated GIF
instead of asking, "How are you?"

Valentine's Day had a budget of $52 million.
I told you I loved you in a Facebook message,

but I wrote it between a joke,
did you notice? When you see Ashton Kutcher

walk into the scene, you know the movie
will be a disappointment.

They met for an "I Hate Valentine's" dinner.
They should have stayed home and finished their laundry.

Sometimes, life feels like
Ashton Kutcher just walked into the scene,

When you leave, when
the plane floats off, and I am still here,

we blister. Or,
we flood.

I'll still be here, when the water damage
crusts, or when we callus.

They confuse the notion of love.
They get it wrong every time.

They spend $52 million getting it
wrong in under two hours.

I am $13.50 divided by $52 million,
or,

what if my dislike of Ashton Kutcher
is just another way to avoid loneliness?

Or, maybe we both relate too much to Anne Hathaway,
because poetry can't pay the bills but the phone sex can.

All the celebrities in the world
can't fix a broken heart,

or, Kathy Bates
just reminds me of *Misery*,

or,
that,

love
is the all-consuming moment

before Ashton Kutcher
walks into the scene.

What's Your Number?

[Opening credits]

Scan over magazines,
headlines about how to fall in love.

> Those love-life instructions induce
> anxiety and confuse so many heroines.

[Intro to leading lady]

Feel slut-shamed by those magazines
and old ladies. Fix hair.

[Meet cute]

Hot neighbour knocks on the door, asks to be let in
while I try to force a hookup to leave.

> If she just embraced her sluttiness
> there'd be a threesome during the end credits.

Vodka pours into the morning and droops
shame as low as his balls.

[Dialogue]

"If you ever want to hook up you can call me."
"No one likes doggy style."

[Character development]

I was growing out my bangs.
I'm always growing out my bangs.

> Bangs are a lesson in patience,
> an important personal test.

[Dialogue]

"Now, thanks to that finger-smelling fuck,
I'm at 20."

> If a magazine tells you that having sex
> with 20 men makes you a monster, burn that magazine.

[Character development]

20 guys is theoretically too many
to have fucked to be marriage material.

> If this was a film about gay men
> 20 would be the virgin's number.

I used to feel hot when I met people I used to date.
Now I just hide behind a cake.

[Musical montage]

"Animal"
by Neon Trees.

Fact: Neon Trees headlined
the *NYLON* and Starbucks Frappuccino Music Tour.

Drinking wine and researching ex-boyfriends online
while listening to the kind of music sold at Starbucks
is actually advisable.

[Dialogue]

"Do you know how exhausting it was to breathe fresh air?"
"The guy who threw up in our dishwasher?"

[Costume]

Why would you wear a pantsuit?
That's the beauty of a pantsuit.
That pantsuit was sexy because it was hard
to tell what was going on underneath the pantsuit.

[Dance interlude]

A bad cover
of "Three Times a Lady."

[Character development]

Just the tip still counts.
Just the tip doesn't count.

No one likes doggy style.

[Big dramatic fight]

Listen, shrivelled vagina, your days are over.
Your little art project can wait, my penis comes first.

Leave in the middle of your sister's wedding
because you have terrible priorities.

[Final speech to proclaim love]

Fuck, fuck, fuckity, fuck, asshole.

[End credits]

"Neon Lights" by Natasha Bedingfield.

Ana Faris and Ari Graynor
deserved a better movie.

She's All That

1

You were a nerd with glasses,
but no one noticed you,
nor bet they could turn you
into the most popular person in school.
You just went on
wearing your glasses,
reading books,
eating tuna sandwiches.

2

The truth is,
if any of this shit happened to you
in real life,
you'd call the cops.

50 First Dates

You sang me a song
but I forgot.

You took me to the aquarium.
I forgot.

Took me on a boat.
Forgot.

I keep watching *The Sixth Sense*,
over and over again, waiting for the twist.

Every morning I wake up on a boat
next to a man

who tells me I love him
on a VHS

but I can't remember.
Now the ocean surrounds me

and I never trusted
the open water.

Line, Please

This is possibly the most adorable creature I've ever been in contact with, and if she turns out to be as good looking as a mailbox … I would be crazy enough to turn my life upside down and marry her.

I'll just be hanging around the mistletoe, hoping to be kissed.

If you find somebody you can love, you can't let that get away.

You said you couldn't be with someone who didn't believe in you. Well I believed in you. I just didn't believe in me. I love you … always.

To some people, love doesn't exist unless you acknowledge it in front of other people.

After all … I'm just a girl, standing in front of a boy, asking him to love her.

Is it still raining? I hadn't noticed.

Shut up, just shut up.

You had me at "hello."

there's something about
there's something about

there's something about

ITS FUNNY
WHAT LOVE
CAN MAKE
YOU DO

there's something about

there's something about

there's something about

there's something about

there's something about
there's something about
there's something about

mary

Unrequited Love

a found Wikipedia poem

1. Classical times – early eighteenth century: General disease caused by unrequited love.
2. Early eighteenth – beginning nineteenth century: Practice of excess physical love (akin to nymphomania or satyriasis).
3. 6 References
4. Condition can be found in the work of Hippocrates, Erasistratus, Plutarch, and Galen[citation needed]. In the psychiatric literature it has been variously called erotic paranoia and erotic self-referent delusions until the common usage of the terms "erotomania" and "de Clérambault's syndrome."
5. The term "erotomania" is often confused with "obsessive love," obsession with unrequited love, or hypersexuality.
6. 3 History[edit]
7. The core symptom of the disorder is that the sufferer holds an unshakable belief that another person is secretly in love with him or her. In some cases, the sufferer may believe several people at once are "secret admirers." The sufferer may also experience other types of delusions concurrently with erotomania, such as delusions of reference, wherein the perceived admirer secretly communicates his or her love by subtle methods such as body posture, arrangement of household objects, and other seemingly innocuous acts (or, if the person is a public figure, through clues in the media).
8. Early nineteenth century – beginning twentieth century: Unrequited love as a form of mental disease.
9. Erotomania is especially in patients with schizophrenia, delusional disorder, or bipolar mania.[1] Any denial of affection by the object of this delusional love is dismissed

by the patient as a ploy to conceal the forbidden love from the rest of the world.[2]

10. The assassination attempt of Ronald Reagan by John Hinckley Jr. was reported to have been driven by an erotomanic fixation on Jodie Foster.[3]

11. Late night TV entertainer David Letterman and former astronaut Story Musgrave were both stalked by Margaret Mary Ray.[4][5]

12. In one case, erotomania was reported in a patient who had undergone surgery for a ruptured cerebral aneurysm.[2]

13. History [hide]

14. Delusional belief of "being loved by someone else."

Unrequited Love 2
Even More Unrequited

a found Wikipedia poem erasure

1. Classical times – love
2. Early eighteenth – physical love
   (nymphomania or satyriasis)
3. 6 References
4. d'amour
   erotic/a
5. Prominent examples
   love
   love
   hypersexuality
   love
6. 3 History
7. core unshakable belief
   love
   secret admirers
   love
   body posture, arrangement of household objects, and
   other seemingly innocuous acts
   (or, if the person is a public figure, through clues in
   the media)
8. Early nineteenth century – love
   love
   admirer
   affection
   special glances, signals, telepathy, or messages through the
   media
   letters, phone calls, gifts, and visits
   affection
   love is a ploy to conceal the forbidden love from the rest
   of the world.[2]

9. 5 Notes
10. fixation.[3]
    cerebral aneurysm.[2]
11. 4 See also
12. Early twentieth century – present: being loved by someone
13. [hide]
14.

Morning Wood
The 40-Year-Old Virgin

Your morning wood wakes up before you do,
tells you to start the day, pisses all
over the bathroom linoleum floor.

Your morning wood cooks
breakfast for one, then rides his bike
to work, checks in, checks out.

Your morning wood mutters when
women ask you questions about
television sets, mumbles answers.

Your morning wood surrounds itself
with plastic men, whose strengths
are mystical, but clear cells contain them.

Your morning wood reminds you
that shame is hermetically
sealed in a box overlooking your bed.

Your friends take vigil around your
morning wood, every night. Pour
drinks down throats as an amen.

Some Like It Hot

But some are very wary of heat, fear
feeling confused by some woman like her,
some blonde, some singer, someone with really
great comedic timing. Some like it flat.
Some men are way too concerned with being
mistaken for a woman, even if
it's on purpose. Some like it insulting.
Some savour the way a saxophone tastes,
compare playing an instrument to
licking pussy. Some men don't use euphemisms.
Some man dressed in demure women's clothing
sails away with a man, wig in hand. Some
woman ends up with the "fuzzy end of
the lollipop." Some sigh. Nobody's perfect.

Romantic Opposites-Attract Comedies
Your preferences created this row.

for Netflix

He's a carnivore and she's a vegetarian: *Meat Cute?*

He's a vampire and you're a young girl: *Sometimes Love Bites.*

She's an executive and he's a plumber: *Plumb Love II.*

They met online, but he doesn't even own a computer: will their binary codes match up? *XOX010*

He's an ex-dinosaur and she's a figment of his imagination: *T. R-ex.*

He's Jennifer Aniston and she's Brad Pitt: *The Love Pitt.*

They met on a cruise and he didn't tell her he was just a crew member: *Lietanic.*

He's a Republican known for his huge penis and she's a Democrat who runs a farm: *Donkey Lover.*

He's a DJ and she's deaf: *I Only Hear You.*

He's a baseball player and she's a reporter: *What Is Glove?*

They meet at the ocean's edge: *There's No Place Like Foam.*

Screwball Mix 'N' Match

BEGINNING

1. An upper-crust private eye
2. A dotty spinster
3. A hapless scientist
4. An unstoppable heiress
5. A runaway socialite
6. A brash sportswriter
7. A headstrong political columnist
8. A love-struck teenager
9. A crooked foursome

MIDDLE

A. is invited to spend the weekend at the estate of a munitions mogul

B. helps lonely old gents by poisoning and then burying them in the cellar

C. whose dog steals his prize dinosaur bone, and her pet leopard is mistaken for a zoo escapee

D. is about to get hitched to a dull insurance agent – that's if her ex-husband, a ruthless newspaper publisher, doesn't succeed in winning her back

E. in a string of zany misadventures that lead them to realize they're madly if reluctantly in love

F. prepares to marry, but her ex and a tabloid reporter have other ideas as they converge on her home for a fateful visit

G. accidentally witness the St. Valentine's Day Massacre, then get out of town the only way they know how: dressed as women

H. trade barbs in print, then meet, fall in love, and walk down the aisle together

I. sneaks into the apartment of playboy artist

J. commits the heist of the century

END

But things heat up on the road when they meet a curvy blonde who plays the ukulele then balancing work and marriage turns out to be a problem and he agrees to date her until her infatuation subsides and soon he's spouting teen slang and she is affecting an air of sophistication and is about to get away with it all until the London Police arrest one of them, but can the three on the lam persuade their comrade's lawyer to reveal the stolen loot's location?

Sex Scene

INT. BEDROOM — NIGHT

An hour or so after MAN and WOMAN have consumed
watery-looking wine.

Dark. So dark. Subtle lighting symbolizes hidden
lust. No one sees. Moans uttered. WOMAN's mouth was
previously spouting off on loneliness. MAN's mouth was
chewing rib-eye.

MAN enters. Or does he? This is rated PG-13. It's so
dark. Heavy breathing. It's a joke. WOMAN flips a light
switch. DOG sits panting heavily. MAN and WOMAN wear
artfully rumpled clothing. They smell of fraud and
regret.

>   MAN
>   You make me want to make love
>   like a better man.

>   WOMAN
>   Make the bed. It's filthy.

Fade out. Because it's not time yet. This is a misstep.
The real sex scene will happen later in a trailer on a
lot with crew smoking nearby.

                                                CUT TO:

EXT. PARK — DAY

Yes. Day. Too light. Too sunshiny for anyone to have a
hard-on.

It's days after they've discovered their friends have
been talking to each other about them.

>   WOMAN
>   I don't feel beautiful and/or sexy for
>   a variety of reasons that are both personal
>   and systemic
>   societal issues.

>   MAN
>   I am going to make mistakes
>   that will make
>   my penis look appealing.

                                                CUT TO:

EXT. MEN'S UNDERPANTS — NIGHT

This is months after a searing misunderstanding between
MAN and WOMAN drove them to opposite corners of the
office.

                                              CUT TO:

EXT. WOMAN'S BRA — NIGHT

One second after the shot of the underpants.

                                              CUT TO:

INT. MAN'S MOUTH — NIGHT

A few seconds after the bra is discreetly removed.

                                              CUT TO:

INT. VAGINA - NO TIME MARKER

No one is allowed to film inside here.

                                              CUT TO:

INT. — NIGHT? SOMETIME LATER IN THE PITCH BLACK

EXT. — TWO PAIRS OF GLISTENING LIPS

INT. — UNIDENTIFIED CROOK IN THE BODY

EXT. — DUVET TOO EXPENSIVE FOR CHARACTER TO AFFORD

INT. — BRAIN — UNSURE OF TIME, CONFUSED

EXT.

INT.

EXT.

                          MAN
                          . . .

                        WOMAN
                          . . .

Fade out. Out of pity. Nothing to see here.

Sex Scene (revision)

INT. BEDROOM — NIGHT

An hour or so after MAN and MAN have consumed
watery-looking wine.

Bright, under the fluorescents.

MAN weaves hand through hair, makes it worse, messes
the comb's work.

>   MAN
>   I'm not clean.

>   MAN
>   I know.

Camera blurs until the only thing in focus is the tele-
vision screen.

>   CUT TO:

A FRUIT BOWL.

Claymation of the banana peeling itself.

>   MAN
>   I'm really into symbolism.

>   MAN
> They based my character on the dad from _____.

>   CUT TO:

EXT. MEN'S UNDERPANTS

>   CUT TO:

EXT. MEN'S UNDERPANTS

>   CUT TO:

EXT. MEN'S UNDERPANTS

>   CUT TO:

JOCKSTRAP.

No one is allowed to film inside here.

>   CUT TO:

INT. — PITCH BLACK

EXT. — PITCH BLACK

INT. — ARMPIT HAIR

EXT. — MEN'S UNDERPANTS

INT. — PITCH BLACK

EXT.

INT.

EXT.

>   MAN
>   (quotes something from *Mean Girls*)

>   MAN
>   I miss Lindsay Lohan.

Fade out. Out of pity.

Your Boobs

must be covered up
must have retractable nipples
must be dealt with in post
must not be seen by teens
must wear a bra during all sex scenes
must be held up by a slightly out-of-date bra
must pretend to find comfort
must appear happy
should bounce around just enough to make them appear happy
should be alluded to
should be invisible
may be used as a comic element
may be used as a sex prop
may give a man a black eye for comedic effect
are abusive
are offensive
are the cause of MPAA ratings restrictions
are changing into fatty monsters
are twisting dicks into fleshy pretzels
are taking down whole cities
are crushing men
are destructive
are great orators capable of compelling other breasts to join
    their cause with powerful speeches, commanding hand
    gestures, and threats of genocide
will increase and decrease in size at will
will increase and decrease in aggression at will
will ruin the world
will cause the end of civilization

Asshole

this is a compliment in the world of romantic comedies
because if you're interesting you must also be full of some-
thing: could be yourself, could be alcohol, could be a
particular feeling like rage or despair or regret and you're
almost certainly full of that hilarious bitterness that affects
people who blame all of their problems on some person who
wronged them, a woman who wanted a hug or a coffee or a
declaration louder than a sigh, or a man who couldn't quite
keep quiet even when the point was not to talk about him-
self or to talk at all, just *full*, and full of excuses for why things
didn't turn out, why they were dumped unceremoniously,
why they are a GOOD GUY, a GOOD GIRL, just human
sphincters holding back so much shit.

How to Lose a Guy in 10 Days, or "Asshole"

Never
call
him
back.

People Are Assholes!

you look so good
that size, that shape,
with that traumatic scar
accentuated, sitting
silent while I neg you
into love

all the things we meant to say,
we mean when we say, we are mean
we crumple our fingers together,
fists not balled, balls are smooth,
these are nobs of flesh pulsing

stupid ugly mean bitch bastard
selfish useless cuts fruit
the wrong way
never does anything
with the toilet seat
closes doors too quickly
has a small dick, brain, career trajectory

quick shots scour,
from the pink of the mouth, travel
like chipped nails
until they catch in our throat

your mother is a monster

your first husband cheated for a reason

everyone you love died because of something you did

someone said, "love means
not ever having to say you're sorry"

what a fucking asshole.

You Did That on Your Own

You were the one who took that nervous elevator ride.
You were the one who purchased Spanx and Crocs.
You misunderstood.
You put your tongue too far down his throat.
You forgot to get gas.
You insulted everyone's best friend.
You peed your pants a little bit, just that one time.
You dated two people at the same time but only
    for three months.
You cut off those jeans into jorts.
You took chances.
You took his childhood teddy bear instead of the blame.
You threw a dozen rotten pears.
You invited everyone to your poetry reading.
You did something to someone else.

Definitely, Maybe

A poetic memoir

One time, you yelled from the bottom
floor that you had feelings for this guy, and he said
"Maybe after Christmas" from his balcony.

One time, you asked a guy out and he said,
"Maybe, but not right now. I went out with
_____ for nine days
and I haven't really recovered."

One time, you asked a guy
for the third date, and the last text
you ever received from him was
"Maybe next week."

One time, a guy was high on MDMA,
shirtless, dancing, sweating.
You asked him if he wanted
to get out of here, and he smiled, said, "Definitely."
He paused, then he said, "Maybe."
He paused again, then said, "Definitely, maybe."

In a Movie about Weddings
No One Wants to Attend

a found poem

I absolutely loved it.
It was great.
It had the right people to play each character.

The acting was
fantastic and the movie
was very entertaining and hillariouse
espesially the part were
that one girl gets her hair died
blue.

When I first saw this movie I was like oh my gosh
this is wonderful but not as great as *twilight*
but I will say that all of the other reviews
are way to mean and harsh.

Do not be a devil.

In a Movie about Weddings
No One Wants to Attend 2
Even Less Interested

an adapted found poem

I absolutely loved it?
It was great?
It had the right people to play each character?

The acting was
fantastic? And the movie
was very entertaining and hilarious?

So I Married a Poet

There was a time when Mike Myers was cute. So cute.

There was a time when Mike Myers was a poet. Wasn't that a funny time?

There was a time when romantic comedies were like jokes about men versus women. They were everywhere.

There was a time when Mike Myers was a poet and the poet made money in the nineties. In the nineties poetry was so hot.

There was a time when if you wanted a fun montage of meat being chopped up by a sexy lady with enormous hair, then you were in luck.

There she goes again!

There was a time before Gerard Butler.

Is it more believable that a poet earned a living wage or that anyone would ever want to have sex with Gerard Butler?

There was a time before Gerard Butler jokes.

There was a time when you could marry a poet and poems had to rhyme:

> *Poet, sweet poet.*
> *You are like beef.*
> *You add a bay leaf.*
> *You make a stew in my heart.*

Funny Face

If you are a bookseller
and you become a model
and get to parade
all over Paris
photographed in couture
the last thing you should do
is fall in love with Fred Astaire
when you could just
get drunk and high
and sing and dance
your way through
a jumping beatnik bar
(especially after the high-high
of a disastrous fashion show)
so don't get married.
Read all the philosophy,
but keep the Givenchy.

But *Hocus Pocus* Isn't Even a Rom Com?

for Charles Demers

Bette Midler put a spell on you, and now you are hers.
The quickest way to a woman's heart is through her yabbos;
your virginity, both a blessing and a curse.

The way you dance until the dawn, it lures,
the same way your head falls off so easily.
Bette Midler put a spell on you, and now you are hers.

You kissed her under the glow of the book. Salt in her purse
couldn't save her from your laid-back Hollywood style:
your virginity both a blessing and a curse.

If you ever figured out that love cures
all failures and errors, welp, apologies to Sarah Jessica Parker,
Bette Midler put a spell on you, and now you are hers.

Max, did you ever take the moment to notice opening
    books ensures
society will fall into the depths of evil,
your virginity, both a blessing and a curse?

Or did you not know that when the time comes
it will all turn to dust: yabbos, cats, and all?
Bette Midler put a spell on you, and now you are hers,
your virginity, both a blessing and a curse.

You Are the Devil, I (Should) Have Said

I keep a list in a pink notebook of cute personal memories. A dream journal of reality. Moments that would make great romantic scenes on film. That time someone pushed his hand under my shirt uninvited and I laughed about it, even though he was insulted, because we were all preteens and watching *Earth Girls Are Easy*. That time the guy with a leather jacket and Dep-gelled hair tried to push me out of a car on the highway because I wasn't being "the one," because his joke wasn't funny. That time that guy yelled at me because, instead of having sex with him on Christmas Eve, I told him I didn't love him, even though he'd made me sign a contract that stated that I would expressly have sex with him as a super-romantic Christmas gift. That time I cried in bed until salt marked red half moons under each eye, until I felt I'd paid for mistakes I wasn't sure about. The scenes before the girl makes up with the guy, before the guy forgives the girl for being a bitch.

Montage

Change clothes, change accessories, change your hairstyle,
change the colour of your hair, change styles, change your
clothes, remove your eyeglasses, bake a cake, bake a cake and
leave it on his doorstep, get your tail lights fixed, look up
all of your exes, look up all of your exes and find out what
they are up to, try all the cakes, try all of the wedding cakes,
change clothes, try on dresses, try on dresses and change
clothes, get your friends to try on dresses, change clothes,
learn to smoke, quit smoking, try all of the cakes, learn a
new skill, learn another new skill, try yoga, finish your opera,
finish your puzzle, walk along the beach, walk through the
city, walk across the entire country, start a business, take
meditation classes, meditate, sit in a swing pensively reflect-
ing on your life, look off-screen with a knowing smile, fade
to the next day.

Romantic Comedies for Young Girls

Hollow Ship to Hell

for Ariel

You saw him on the ship
destined to wreck.
Pulled him from the flames
and laid his body to beach.

I was a fish once too,
fins for feet, flapping on the beach only for moments
before the air burned my skin.

So I slit my body in half,
cut my flesh into two feet, and
placed myself into his life
at every moment to catch
his attention.

One day, my body began to seal itself.
Skin tightened and my gills
grew back. I was up late one night in his bed
and the air began to burn my skin
again, my body craving the ocean.

Now, he cuts his skin to create gills
but can never stay under water long enough
to keep from floating upwards.

Tries to weight himself with concrete,
tries to anchor.

The Rose

for Belle

What happens after
you suffer through
beasts and a wedding,
everyone you knew
changed into old flesh?

You were so smart. I always thought
it was about books, ideas,
stories, adventure, living life
through the eyes of another,
pretending because life
wasn't so fucking great.

I'd been dismissed too
for talking about thinking,
pressing my nose to books,
creating new spaces in my body
for knowledge.

When you're young
all the sexy misogynists,
provincial gym monkeys
show off their brawn.
Their triangle torsos
look just like a beast's.

Maybe Stockholm Syndrome
isn't any less romantic
than cocktease guilt?

But once you got involved in your own fairy tale,
it's so meta, the magical rose,
like the kind ladies throw
to knights, like the kind
someone in a different story
will compare to your vagina.

Those stories are outdated.

What happens when
you're crafted into delicate stained glass,
when you've transformed
into something flat and lifeless?

YOU CANT
ALWAYS RUN
FROM YOUR
PAST

Emotionally Broken

Romantic comedies are dead because we're emotionally broken.

Romantic comedies are dead because romance is dead.

Romantic comedies are dead because everyone is fulfilled.

Romantic comedies are dead because no one reads
poetry anymore.

Romantic comedies are dead because the government decided
to kill them.

Romantic comedies are dead because of the word "bromance."

Romantic comedies are dead because of the word "sext."

Romantic comedies are dead because someone's mother
watches the W Network on mute.

Romantic comedies are dead because *What Women Want*.

Romantic comedies are dead because there is no way anyone
could love Bradley Cooper.

Romantic comedies are dead because pyrotechnicians rule the
world, litter occasions with fireworks.

Romantic comedies are dead because Nora Ephron is dead.

Romantic comedies are dead because Reese Witherspoon
won an Oscar.

Romantic comedies are dead because box office is our metric,
our soulmate, our hollow ship to Hell.

Because You Watched *27 Dresses*

You wait for men on towers
or hesitate just before the moment you

board the plane. You become his assistant and quit
when he is fired. You go to 27 weddings and work

for the prime minister of England. You lose your husband
and spend years following his letters from the grave

chasing your grief around the world to only realize you
should have been
making shoes. You open up a small bookshop next to a
large corporate

bookstore that sells mainly soaps and candles. You become a
reporter who masquerades
as a young teen in high school to sell a story about what's
cool. You let depression sink

into your body, purchase the most expensive bedsheets, pay
for the most high-profile therapist you can find, who
helps you start a new business so you can continue to
credit-card your sorrow away.

Overboard

Even an heiress with amnesia
falls in love with a sea dog
and his rough craft, four sons
and being poor, working hard.

The message is always:
Don't be scared of falling
because you'll land
in sexy arms of love.

And you might. Your torso
might press into another's,
your mouths might mash
together, your parts might bump

to orgasm. You'll end up
entwined like a sailor's knot,
duped into believing in another life,
because you don't recall owning a yacht.

Being scared
doesn't mean you won't find
love, lust, a torso to rest
your body parts on.

Stay wary. Love changes,
abandons you in a small-town
hospital to party with barely legals.
Our brains fail us at the best of times.

Your body can take chances,
can function upright or fallen down.
Don't think, move. Reclaim your yacht.
Steady now. You're steering yourself.

He's Just Not That into You

Not that he's just into you.
He just wants to get into you.

I Am So Lonely, I Am So Fucking Lonely, lol, SEND, *Obvious Child*

for Gabe Liedman

I

I'm onstage, and crickets deafen
ears and tumbleweeds roll
around me, he left, and they
build love around puppies

and a home, and I am a piece
of shit, here I am, a big piece
of shit. I tweet, I am so miserable
lol, SEND. I tweet, where

are you when I need you, lol,
SEND. I refresh pages,
delete history, empty trash
bins, drink all the fucking

white wine my white body
can handle. Break. Like
a condom. Break. Like
wind. What if love was

the warm intensity of
a fart in your face?

2

What if the camera moves a little
to the left, and it just stays on you?
What if this is the rom com, and it's
just me and you? what if geographic

distance wasn't real? What if the daggers
you stare with, those who fall for each
other, what if they are so lonely,
lol, what if you are the main

character, and the movie
has just begun?

He Grasps at Emotion, or *The Proposal*

for Sandra Bullock

The family asks you to tell them about the proposal, how he did it, and you make up a lie on the spot. But it isn't easy for you. You know what it would be like if he was real and if he asked you the way you wanted.

You would be watching a movie in the park, and it would be something like *Pretty Woman*. He would turn to you and say, "Let's do this every year, for the rest of our lives." Small tumblers of wine clinking, the wind congratulates you. A small constellation of kisses make out the night as Kit hollers "Cinder-fucking-rella" and that's exactly how it all feels. You would say to yourself, "This is what people talk about when they talk about 'happy'."

But you aren't in a park, and *Pretty Woman* is just a movie. You ball up your emotions the way you always do and carry them in a large Louis Vuitton satchel that drags behind. You bundle it all up again, because you prefer the feeling of safety, and you were never good at uncertainty, but you go through psychology tests every night before you go to bed, because you're not sure you feel anything at all.

You're Supposed to Be Engaged

for Cher

A meat slicer can be an aphrodisiac. Even when you're supposed to be engaged. Especially then. Everyone thinks you're too old to start again. But you're a 37-year-old goddamn widow and the edict is clear: grey hair, big sweaters, Nonna-style on this upcoming, your second, marriage. But the meat slicer. The slim cuts. The wooden hand. Something about the contrast of wobbly deli meat and hard lumber. So many euphemisms together. Your fiancé proposed in a hurry before flying to his dying mother. When death in Sicily calls, all mama's boys must answer. I always thought it strange that no one understood that you were better than all of them until you fucked Nicholas Cage and dyed your hair goth black. Fluffing a perm, however, is always an indication that a woman is in full bloom. So you're supposed to be engaged. So what? You can do whatever you want. Call men wolves because they are, retell their stories for them because they've changed their narratives, victimized beyond repair. You're supposed to be engaged but you cheat. Your fiancé breaks it off, not because you cheated, but because he's superstitious. The mama's boy's mama will die if you wed. That's not love. Who wants a freak like that anyway? There are better freaks. You're supposed to be engaged, but you changed your mind.

Puff Puff, Give. Puff Puff, Give

I
always
thought
Friday
was
a
very
romantic
comedy
about
Ice
Cube
and
Chris
Tucker
trying
to
have
a
threesome
with
a
joint.

Acting

It's in the shoulders
and the lips. Anything
can shrug. Wrists
roll into suit pockets,
sly indicators of interest.
Pupils roll around
in all directions,
make everyone dizzy.
Including yourself.
Blink to tears. Blink
them back. And do it again
with a happy feeling.
Blink. No, wink. Pretend
you don't even
have eyes. Attempt
contact. But
don't. Look away
if someone looks at you.
If you're alone
you can sigh. Stumble
in heels, stumble
in flats, stumble into arms,
retract your whole body.
Clamp down tongue,
hands, thoughts, nipples,
anything
that will give you away
as someone who really wants.

The Acting Was Fantastic

I pretended to like the movie
so we could make out.

Forgetting Sarah Marshall

1

Did you remember the way love works? I told you once
in a small elevator that the world closes in on you in the
moments of memory. Sometimes I work on forgetting.
I practise it every five minutes. I work through each
memory of you, and forget that one, then move onto the
next. Sometimes it all comes back, and I work on blacking
it out, from the couch, to the bed, to the television, to the
chicken sandwich you ate afterwards. Ashes have memories
attached too, but you can't see them. Jumping off a cliff
doesn't make them run away, it only lets it slip back until
the memory jumps too, and holds onto you for dear life in
the ocean that was never very good at swallowing you up.
The ocean runs away from you too.

2

Sometimes I think about how thoughts of you stretch my
skin. You have a terrible memory so you smile more than
I do. I remember, one time in Hawaii, you tightened the
blankets around my body so I couldn't escape, or so that
memory couldn't escape, and you put a bible over my chest.
I don't believe in monsters, so I slipped away in the night.

3

You are the devil, I said. Blond hair and blue eyes. I gave you
control. I gave up all control. Control is just a construct. I
gave up my memories. I figured I could try again, start with
new ones, so I handed them to you, but you were never very
good at carrying things. I gave my memories names, and put
them on your shoulders. I buried a few for later. I put some
of them, the ones that sweeten from nostalgia, in Mason jars
and leave them in the cupboard, then put a few of them on
the counter because they look better for public display.

4

You said jump, and I did. The memory holding on for dear life.

You Fell for the Wrong Girl

Her face glossy
easy, breezy, beautiful.
That face glued on a billboard,
the best features
of another woman
glued to her skin. Eyes
that pop like *Pygmalion*'s
boner for shapely ivory.
Breasts as lovely and temperate
as barely legal Scarlett Johansson's.
Her nooks are perfume-sample sweet.
Everything aligned. Legs
mannequin slick.
You see the world
through Kim Cattrall's
thigh-gap, reach
for a sculpted navel.
Two teens can make a woman
Kelly Le Brock-bodacious
out of masturbation
perspiration, a Barbie doll,
and weird science.
Keep adding breasts,
a second or third vagina.
She is *Her*, a voice designed
to deliver smooth gratification.
But still, something is off.
Maybe she's wrong, because
she doesn't push herself
hard enough to be a real girl.
Or maybe it's your fault
you don't look like Ryan Gosling.

But Maybe He Wasn't Really a Person

You watch too many romantic comedies so you stayed with the
   wrong guy
for the story. For the narrative. He fit the scenario you created,
and the stories you build wrap a theatre around your heart.

You couldn't get out of bed the day he left, put beer in your
   coffee cup,
and told everyone you were moving to Bali.
You watch too many romantic comedies so you stayed with
   the wrong guy.

You created a narrative between text messages and between
things that were unspoken, that maybe were never real,
and the stories you build wrap a theatre around your heart.

You moved across the country to live with him
and when you showed up to his apartment unannounced he
   said "Oh."
You watch too many romantic comedies so you stayed with the
   wrong guy.

You flirted with a guy via Twitter who said he was James Franco,
you sent him your number not realizing it was a robot,
and the stories you build wrap a theatre around your heart.

Before you go to bed, you imagine him leaving his wife, maybe at
a dinner party with all of his famous friends, falling asleep to your
   own dream.
You watch too many romantic comedies so you stayed with the
   wrong guy
and the stories you build wrap a theatre around your heart.

On Every Television Channel

On every television channel
there's an opportunity for viewing
modern takes on Shakespeare, no period
costumes or iambic pentameter.
Who needs it when you can have Heath Ledger
and his greasy 90s curls, put-downs, come-ons,
crooning. He can't take his eyes off of you.
The football field is so American,
so glowy your head feels like a pompom.
This is a movie about teens, for you,
even though it's not how romance works out.
Or did you not know that when the time comes
your only choice will be to wait and wait
for grand gestures that don't materialize?

This Is Considered Adorable

You lost it all in the recession,
wrote the sorrow in a diary,
called a young girl a cunt.
You fell for the wrong guy.

She bought you containers for your cereal.
Lucky Charms choke, said, "There's someone else"
in the living room, naked.
You fell for the wrong girl.

He broke your car seat, he broke
your mirror, he broke your bed frame,
he broke wind, and this was considered adorable.
You fell for the wrong guy.

You placed your hope in a song,
let the world pass you by, paid
your dues in meatballs.
You fell for the wrong girl.

He left you when he was accepted
into law school, you tried to
win hearts, trading pink for black.
You fell for the wrong guy.

Titanic

What if *Titanic* was just a romantic comedy
starring Leonardo DiCaprio and the Ocean?

The Stories You Build

The stories you build feel
real. Not just onscreen,
in you. Stories pile
in the rational parts of your brain.

Transformative, life-solving
love. Eyes stare into eyes
until misunderstandings break
your slobbering bodies apart.

Mistakes atoned for
in specific gifts, boom boxes
blaring, iconic buildings
illuminated, Tic Tacs.

You want overtures
that could get someone
put in jail: an airport-gate crash,
a jewel theft, some wholesome kidnapping.

He will come to you
without asking when
you need saving, when
he doesn't even know where you are.

Nora Ephron

She wasn't your best friend,
but she could've been.

The advice would have blown down
your door, rearranged your meagre apartment.

You would have felt better
about almost everything,

though sometimes not the endings
of stories. Those would leave you confused.

Like, why doesn't anyone question
the love-of-your-life conceit?

Why can't a story end
with solo wine, torn T-shirt, underpants?

That's comfort. But so is she.
Writing desires, making things messy, then tidy.

She wasn't your best friend,
She could've been anyone's.

She was everyone's.

Ever Wondered If You Might Be
the Best Friend of a Romantic Lead?

(Additionally, you might be quirky.)

FIND OUT NOW!

Check all that might apply:

❑ Zooey Deschanel might wear a kitten / panda / owl cardigan to play you.

❑ You use words that make your sexually active friends cringe.

❑ When you take off your pants and your underpants there is a second pair of underpants painted onto your body.

❑ You tell everyone you are married to one-liners.

❑ When you cry alone a ukulele soundtrack plays every single time.

❑ You have never heard a saxophone sound sincerely sexy.

❑ You shave your legs, but only because you can't bear the scratchy feeling. It's just so … adult.

❑ You're always available by phone for long discussions of other's sex problems, heart problems, brain problems.

❑ Your inner life is unknown to even your Instagram followers.

❑ No one takes your advice seriously.

❑ Every encounter is an opportunity for a joke.

❑ You joke because you're so used to that role.

❑ You're used to it because no one listened when you tried to be serious.

❑ No one takes your advice seriously.

❑ You're not sure if your friends really like you.

❑ You're pretty sure you'll never find love.

❑ Every time you order a vibrator online you open the box and the contents have turned into sparkly dust.

Sonnets for Supporting Roles

Rita, *Bridesmaids*

One morning, you took a towel out of your
son's drawer and its softness had turned
to stone. As you tried to press it into the
washing machine, it cracked in half. The way you

feel when the night comes and this isn't
anything you expected. When she walks
down the aisle, you think about it all over
again, what falling in love is like: the warm

way bodies shake with new desire.
When she tells you that you are more
beautiful than Cinderella, you remember
the way it all began. The way he spent

his time fighting for your attention, the
way you let him, the way you gave in.

Dionne, *Clueless*

The way you let him, the way you gave in
still doesn't make the neighbourhood
feel like home. When the picture is taken, you
are to the far left, or the far right,

not centre. You didn't want to be called woman
knowing what that really means, knowing
the slang slides down your skin that
isn't the colour of hers.

If you spend your days being a sidekick
if you help her get her driver's licence
if you help her get a boyfriend, if you
focus on being the other for others

maybe you will be voted most popular and
that, maybe, it could happen to you.

Muriel, *It Could Happen to You*

That, maybe, it could happen to you,
another working-class woman can swoop in
take your husband who was always
more infatuated with your womb

than with your fire. Someone gives
you a way out, a golden ticket, a hand
never offered. They see you as "other"
and that makes them uncomfortable,

your desire to escape the low income
that you were forced into. "You so stupid,"
you cry out, as he slips away, to a world
where women are as white as the cream

they serve him with coffee. This world isn't
for you, not for you, but for porcelain dolls.

George, *My Best Friend's Wedding*

For you, not for you, but for porcelain dolls
walking down the aisle. You are a cellphone
or an emergency lip gloss. You are the touch-up
rouge in her purse, you are the gay best friend.

The one who fusses over her hair, memorizes wardrobe,
waits in your apartment for whenever she is ready.
Filing nails, and sitting on your Barcelona chair,
watching *Murder, She Wrote* until she calls.

When she is ready, you snap fingers and make
jokes with flapping hands, tell her she has it all.
When she needed you most, you flew down
to save a dance at the wedding, a wedding you

could never have, legally, so instead you collapsed
back into a lipstick and a clasp purse.

Kit, *Pretty Woman*

Back into a lipstick and a clasp purse,
where you keep your drugs, and your condoms.
She would sometimes get the higher-
class gentleman, but you're not what

they are looking for, or so you say. You don't
get to be Cinder-fucking-rella. Your glass slipper
has burn-marked edges from the crystal.
You offer a night to a grandpa and say

his wife can watch for extra, and it's laughed
off, but you need the money, your life
depends on the kindness of strangers
or else your moth wings burn in neon red light.

When you watch her taken away in her carriage
it all sinks in a bit deeper, breaking the skin.

Christmas

for Daniel Zomparelli

Christmas is supposed to be
about love, or about the other.

About the way we're supposed
to feel the pull of others to us,

and I guess us to them. We want
holiday-movie elation.

Liam Neeson is a sad miracle. Emma Thompson
is the part of you it hurts to see. Don't

even get me started on Keira Knightley. Some characters
are always worshipped for no good reason.

What is the anatomy of a Christmas movie?
It's a human shape that wears novelty sweaters

and drinks eggnog. You drink too much
and hope that the cute guy notices

how loud and funny your jokes are,
even though you're going to offend

his best friend in ten minutes
by being right about how offensive he is.

Sad faces look at mistletoe
and, below, incessant kissing;

slobbering fools, happy couples,
mismatched lovers. Even

when you know love
is really holes in underwear,

and shared silence. Small efforts
warm your heart the most,

death, sickness, forgetting how you used to be
as a kid on Christmas, a hopeful teen. Somehow

we all end up like Laura Linney,
unable to fulfill our own Christmas wish lists.

What we need to do is gather around a screen
with full bottles of wine,

and watch a fuck-load of celebrities
make merry, break hearts,

become barometers of holiday cheer.
Because it's all about tradition.

You decorate with a remote control
and turn on the television.

Love Actually

Love, actually
moves between the spaces of desire and fulfillment, it isn't
the spaces of longevity versus
boredom, between
sustainability and perpetual validation, in an ever decreasing
power, love, actually
cannot represent the general public,
love, actually is Mr. Bean selling you jewellery in a bag that
is never
ready for consumption,
love, actually is not
your co-worker, or
your best friend's wife, or
your busty assistant, or
your failed career,
or love is, actually
your failed career,
your busty assistant, or
your best friend's wife, or
your co-worker, or
love, actually is not
ready for consumption,
is never
love, actually is Mr. Bean selling you jewellery in a bag that
cannot represent the general public,
power, love, actually
sustainability and perpetual validation, in an ever decreasing
boredom, between
the spaces of longevity versus
moves between the spaces of desire and fulfillment, it isn't
Love, actually?

When Harry Met Sally

for Cara Ng

1

I don't remember meeting, or if we were really friends.
That's what I want to remember. I know other things: the
soft tonguing of bread before you bit into a sandwich, the
bright flashes before waking next to you, and you floating
down from the tallest building I can imagine. But blockages
compromise. Men and women can't be friends. And can
be friends. It depends on the man and woman. It depends
on how badly that man thinks his dick deserves to plug a
woman. If his only goal in life is to never see the light in the
eyes of someone outside of sex. It depends on how much
you reminisce. It depends if the meeting felt like it took
place in a conference room. No one declares a list that opens
with *I love you because*, no one can stop and start their life.
People forget the beginnings. I want to appreciate why this
feeling is familiar, why I forget.

2

Sometimes I think about trying to get back to a feeling. But
it's so far away I don't know how I'll ever be able to recreate
it. Instead I light 20 cigarettes, lay them in the snow around
me, and try to smoke them all before they melt into their
holes, until my head is so light this feeling dissipates.

3

What if Harry didn't meet anyone? What if Sally met Harry?
What if switching words would transform the outcome
so drastically that Bruno Kirby played the leading man he
deserved to be? What if all that cute stuff was with me and
Bruno Kirby, the two of us stealing scenes and each other's
hearts and maybe pies from windowsills. His moustache
brushing against me. This is why there's entertainment,
escape, fantasy. I can revel in the forgetting and relive
meetups in my mind. To me they're real. Bruno Kirby
watching me fake an orgasm and commending me on my
skills, laughing along, acknowledging me as clever, sexual,
complicated. Not an insult. Bruno reassuring me that I could
be out there, but he's here. I will meow for him. Bruno
keeping up with me. Bruno. Kirby. Breathless.

4

You said we were never friends and we will never be lovers
and we are nothing to each other and it was easy to believe
you. It was easy.

Five-Star Rating

Blindsides you with its charm. As ephemeral as a talk show. Meg Ryan. Haltingly absurd. Smart, sexy, and other dating clichés. Early animosity leads to a predictable ending. A modern take on something else. A series of misunderstandings and soiled T-shirts. Unreal dialogue, wardrobe choices. Love and hate in equal measure. Bristles with implausibility. Literally heartbreaking. Literally heartwarming. Literally vomit-inducing. Pulses. Laughs in your face. Banal. Just like real relationships. Sets up unrealistic expectations. Doesn't hold a candle to plot devices. A tale as old as times you don't remember and references at least two years too old. Some ugly person steals the show. Absent of Meg Ryan. Thumbs-up because they're broken. Puns. Assembly-line epiphanies. Where is Meg Ryan?

The Movie Will Be a Disappointment

What's happening
onscreen isn't relatable.

These people are moving
around too much.

Bodies in motion, kissing,
frolicking, trying.

Why is no one in the corner
crying, covered in spit,

in nostalgia, in blankets
sweat-glued to old T-shirts

melded to a body that hasn't moved
in days and days? Why is no one

covered in a protective shell,
hooded in a paranoid stasis?

The part that makes sense
comes before the movie

bashes us in the face and ears, before
even the ads, quizzes, trailers,

stuff to make us care
about movies. The part

where someone spends too much
on popcorn, butter, chocolate,

soda the size of 20 hearts, before
stepping into a dark room to forget.

What's Happening Onscreen
Isn't Relatable

No one ever flew through traffic and stopped you
from getting on that plane. No one ever ran after you

down the street to tell you they love you.
No one held a boom box outside

your window. No one flew across the world
for you. No one wrote you a song.

No one wrote you a poem. No one followed you
to Rome or pretended to be the man you were looking for.

No one took a bet on you. No one tried to lose
you. No one gave up their job for you.

No one wrote an article about you and fell
in love in the process. No one showed up

at your apartment and climbed the fire escape.
No one recruited David Bowie to sing to you on an airplane.

Someone did kiss you during a sunset,
pulling you in as night pulled the sun down.

But he's gone now, and so is the sunset. And
no one ever lifted you out of bed

when you drank until sorrow melted
off your skin, frost turned to beads of spring,

sorrys dripping from sweat, fever
still telling you something is wrong.

Harold and Maude

for Laura Matwichuck

> *The earth is my body; my head is in the stars.*
> — Maude

Common ground. Dirt.
Love can grow in the dust-up
of a car crashing over a cliff,
the forced peace of a gravesite.
Find the things that might make
another person unhappy,
that make this person
want to toss their arms around you.
Lessons she weaves
out of long silver braids.
She makes magic from reality,
silk scarves adorning
a 79-year-old body. Young women
are too scared to face black humour,
existentialist self-immolation,
consensual, sensual May-December.
Enjoy life through culture, not marriage,
fight for kisses and thievery.
Not harsh, but radical. She's gentle,
breaks down flower metaphors
without being trite.
She makes us root for death.

New Year's Eve

is a poor (wo)man's
Valentine's Day

which is a poor (wo)man's
Love Actually

which is fucking poor.

Don't bother
trying to force
your tongue
down
someone's throat
at midnight.

Don't watch this movie, either.

Soundtrack

If he plays that song that means we're going to be together forever; if he plays the other I'll wilt into the pavement, if he stops at the chorus I'll turn to goo and live in the sewers with cartoon turtles. If the album from seventh grade plays, the heartbreak will look like it did then: tiny bathroom stalls full of tissue bouquets soaked in tears, a first period just before first period, mean girls bitching about your sadness ruining their day. If that song comes on while we're walking into a Moxie's, our wedding will be in the spring surrounded by peonies and anthropomorphic squirrels; but if it's Burger King then he takes out a hollow sparrow, stuffs it full of locks of my hair, and begs it to fly, fly away while I stand by watching and saying over and over, "It's dead, it's over."

Everything Is Bad Choices
that Make Me Feel Good

1

Start with sex. With acrobatic, cup-my-balls sex.
When morning comes after he does, exit.

You could do an impression of a penis, elbows
jutting out, one eye closed; if you practise

enough, you can really shape your
arms to be balls, and look like a dick.

All retail jobs are about discreetly revealing lifelong
problems to strangers, so you can try it at work.

Your co-worker looks like a Noxema girl,
while you get better at looking like a penis.

2

When you came along, dancing on painted white road
lines to prove sobriety, I ticketed

you, but ripped it up. You had more than
a broken tail light, wormy-face, broken

hearted. When you caught me behind the glass
of the corner-store fridge with my bag of carrots

I thought about the way the cold
from the fridge feels familiar, the late

nights of insomnia, for all of the times
we couldn't figure it out. When you

woke up in my bed, I pushed you the way I always do,
triggering your failed love. Now you drive

past my house in the night, your car
a ghost, haunting the street,

until you left me a cake in the shape
of a carrot, with the words "I'm sorry" iced on top.

3

I think about which is more pathetic: solo
baking or a broken bakery dream; or

fucking a handsome wiener
versus dating a monogamous worm-face.

Everything is bad choices that make me feel good
for a time, or good choices that confuse. Even a meal

isn't simple, nor is choosing a dress. Classy-shit
bridal shops produce severe anxiety, sweaty memories.

Sometimes proving a point
is more important than facing the truth,

even if being right means diarrhea. Even if it means losing
love, a best friend, lunch. Going broke

as a bridesmaid is par for the course;
moving in with your mom is optional, but

being confronted with flour, eggs, butter, and dreams –
that ruins a solid night of fun.

4

Punch a giant cookie, your rage
the shade of a bleached asshole.

When you hit bottom, you were greasy hair,
you were a sad Muppet penis in sweatpants.

Sometimes sanity is a woman who's stolen
a litter of puppies breaking you open on a couch,

forcing you to fight. You had to unfurl arms, unball
fists to stop shaping yourself like a dick,

and slap life back. Leave a cake on life's doorstep, fix your
tail lights and wash your hair, stay.

5

Hold on for one more day.

Credits

Dreamland: "A Series of Romantic Comedies That Could Never Be Made," ed. Jeremy Stewart

Matrix: "Five-Star Rating," ed. Jon Paul Fiorentino

Matrix: "How to Lose a Guy in 10 Days" and "She's All That," ed. Leah Horlick and Billeh Nickerson

New Poetry: "Romantic Comedies for Young Girls," ed. George Murray

Plenitude: "Forgetting Sarah Marshall," ed. Matthew Walsh and Andrea Routley

Editor
Sachiko Murakami

Trailer Director
Shay Wilson

Photography
Tina Kulic

Illustrations
Alana Green

Marketing
Zoe Grams
Megan Jones

The Talon Team
Kevin Williams
Ann-Marie Metten
Chloë Filson
Les Smith
Spencer Williams
Greg Gibson
Vicki Williams

With special thanks
to our friends and family, to our many mentors, and to our past and current lovers.

Blooper Reel

You had me at hello, this cinder-fucking-rella
date that never ended. 50 of them to be exact, it
wasn't until the wedding was cancelled, you
left, beds are meant for bodies to be
lifted out of. I can't live without you, or
complete yourself, break up in the right
direction, you're just a virgin, fill the parts
of your body with other men, ones who
wink when you fall, ones who can sew
stories or dip bodies and dance on stars.
You sink into a bathtub, frothy bubbles
coat your body, your love, your ki–ki–ki–kiss.
Sweet home wherever–the–fuck–you–are
when you bend and snap, dream
of the man in the moon, the only man
who's not a true commitment–phobe.
We all go through phases when we question
our own commitment to Reese. We come back around.
Just like after the fight, the breakdown
over something slight that upsets feelings
like a tipped cow. So, my boyfriend died
but he came back to life and wants to get together,
I just really thought I would be able to
spell my way out of this one. If I imagined
my perfect husband, he would have the face
of Ryan Gosling, the body of Ryan Reynolds, the smile
of Ryan Phillippe, but the spirit of Meg Ryan.
One time I was in a romantic comedy
with someone over email exchanges, he was a
prince, but he took all of the money from my
bank accounts and never called back.
Love is feral, I fear Will Ferrell in my dreams, fear
love isn't something for everyone, Farrah Fawcett

feathered hair filling my lungs when you speak
of forever. Someone bought a flight and a fancy
hotel room to see me, and I still think about
how I never saved you from depression. Marisa Tomei
couldn't help but fall for Robert Downey Jr. in Rome
because substance abuse feels like love.
True, sad me, that felt no, like no
no one would airport-love me the way
baggage claim does. Two, had me, at below
the moonlight, he said there was a condom
remember how love is a broken condom. You,
bad me, that yellow stain around my fingers
from chain-smoking. Learn to be more indifferent
than other girls. Like, duh. Romance makes
you feel so stupid. Like, why? Like, what? Like, who
the hell is this guy standing in front of a girl
when the girl is me and all I really want
is to forget being sad is a thing that might happen.
It's so like me, shoving slice after slice
of pizza in my face with mystical intentions
even though I only believe in the higher power
of Kristen Wiig. I love my own hair,
thick like The Rock's arms, shiny like Gwyneth's
face, healthy like my hatred for Ashton Kutcher.
Extensions of us sit waiting to make out,
brush lips and moustaches, in some swish set-decorated
house so unaffordable, unattainable. Not messed up.
Dirty underwear the reality of a day spent being alive,
also, the contents of your misfiring man-brain,
body sludge, goo. It wasn't obvious to you
that my discomfort wasn't love, because you
didn't catch on I was uncomfortable at all.
Bitch face, stink eye, ignore-you-blank-stare,
none of it indicated how clearly I wanted
you to step back, off, under a train.

So obvious that Jenny Slate is my one true pairing.
A pair of shoes won't make it any easier to have sex
in any city. Tottering along in love is to be unbalanced,
to forget. Why am I here again? That old thing again
with problematic memory stuff. Awkward love confessions
in real life are things people want to forget. In movies
everyone is AWWWWing hard on the inside. I want to be kissed
outside of even gross places – dumpsters, steak houses, banks.
Money tricks girls like me for the first two acts. Two
weeks' notice for your job, but men
want to turn women into buildings that they
build up and tear down. Hugh had me; that fellow
knew all the right words in an English accent. He
left his job for me, changed his cheating ways, now
builds community centres for my vagina. *Working Girl*
is the one time the executive and the secretary
should have swept important papers, nameplates,
monogrammed pens and all the business
from the mahogany desk. YOU ARE A MAN,
he says to Amanda Bynes. A man, duh, I get it!
This was supposed to be about
becoming great at college-level North American soccer,
so that you could go on to great things such as
low-level leagues that pay well
below minimum wage, but you fell in love.
"Conan O'Brien looks like a carrot." That's a double negative.
You're a double negative. Belief in a soulmate so that
maybe there is only one in seven billion.
Crazy. We meet around a bar, soak
up divorce. Hey girl, gender is a construct, heartbreak
is better than cancer. We all fall in love, like assholes.
Work *Dirty Dancing* into the conversation: Lift me.
Cafés and diners, people meet there
to do obvious things: eat, talk, feel disappointed.
A screaming woman downs mouthfuls

of pot pie, makes a scene. In the end I always say,
"I'll have what she's having." What might happen
to a person who rejects a ticking clock,
a romantic time bomb, a white tablecloth.
Because you're a goofball. Like, the real kind.
Not Jennifer Aniston flipping her perfect hair
into a perfect pratfall into a perfect pec.
You need abs to love. You need abs to be loved.
To clarify, not just abs, we all have some
abs underneath, all up in there, but you need
visible abs. Abs that cut glass
and grate cheese over nachos you won't eat,
abs that heal the sick and send life-saving injections
to countries you don't know how to spell correctly.
At night I cry out, "Where is my Mark Darcy?"
Straight, awkward men in indies are always afraid to be called
faggot, like the world has limits on them. I only listen to
   vinyl. I watched
the depression montage for one minute, which compared
to my life is the equivalent of ten years. The perks of being
a wallflower is writing poetry no one likes. Sup?
   Nothing, what's
up with you? Nothing. You can't fill in the spaces he cuts
himself. "You put the ass in class." When the apocalypse came
I was only worried about Twinkies and an amusement park.
Singing, "I wanna grow old with you." If you watch this movie
backwards, I will walk out of your life and onto the streets.

Dina Del Bucchia is the author of *Coping with Emotions and Otters* (Talonbooks, 2013) and *Blind Items* (Insomniac Press, 2014). She guest edited the Humour issue of *Poetry Is Dead* magazine and is the artistic director of the Real Vancouver Writers' Series. Her story "Under the 'I'" was a finalist for the RBC Bronwen Wallace Award. Dina co-hosts the podcast Can't Lit with Daniel Zomparelli. She holds an MFA from the University of British Columbia and lives in Vancouver.

Daniel Zomparelli is editor-in-chief of *Poetry Is Dead* magazine, a semi-annual publication devoted to poetry in Canada. He is a co-podcaster at Can't Lit, a monthly webcast on all things Canadian and literature. His first book of poems, *Davie Street Translations* (2012), was published by Talonbooks. Current endeavours include After You, a series of interconnected poems that span North America.

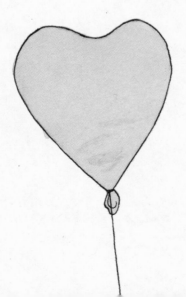